50 NO-NONSENSE WAYS TO INCREASE YOUR SALES TODAY

Are you tired of sales gimmicks that don't work?

Tired of hiring experts for thousands of dollars just to boost your sales?

Then maybe it's time to take matters into your own hands.

This new book simplifies the marketing process so you can start growing

your sales TODAY!

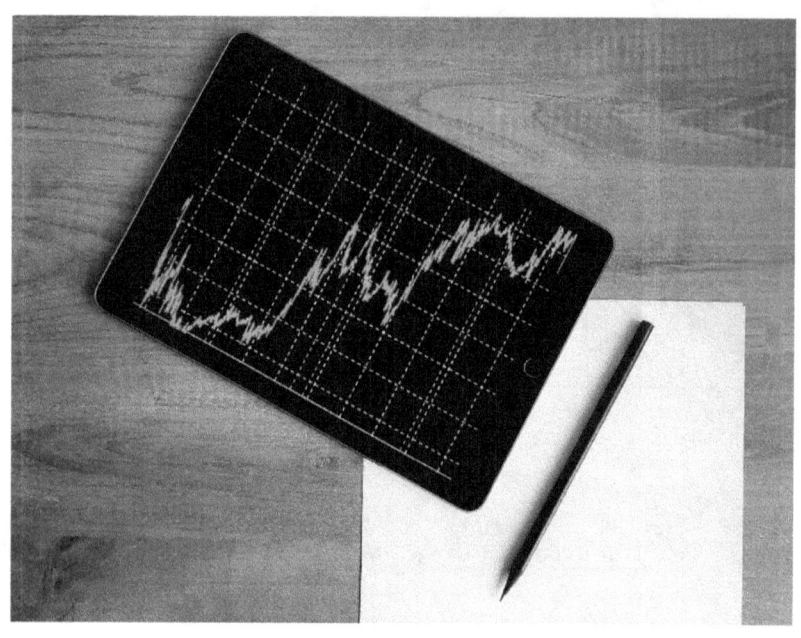

Before you dive into this book, be sure to claim your Free Bonus: Free Traffic Training on How to Get Tons of Traffic to Your Website Without All the Complicated SEO:

http://tiny.cc/se9kgy

In this Free Traffic Training, you will learn how to:
• Instantly get traffic in ANY niche
• Get free exposure from page one of Google, Yahoo, and Bing in 7 minutes or less

- Quickly and easily find people looking to buy what you could be selling
- How to target the traffic that brings in the money instead of fighting over the junk traffic that 99% of everyone else is going for.
- And lots, lots more!

Bonus Number 2 – A Free Life Changing Webinar

If you got shown a simple 3 step process that people like you are using to afford luxury travel worldwide, to make money and to further build their networks, you would have a look right?

Discover how normal people, just like you, are using a simple 3 step formula to create their dream lifestyle online.

You will discover the only 4 things that you need to virtually GUARANTEE your success inside of your business.

www.robertsmallbone.com

In the first 5 minutes you will discover the REAL reason that you might be struggling in your business now & how to avoid all of the major challenges that you're facing inside of your business today.

By the end of this webinar you will 100% understand how to get from where you are now to where you want to go, FAST!

This webinar will open your eyes to a whole new world and will provide you with an incredible platform to achieving the ultimate travel and business lifestyle. The true laptop lifestyle. Click on the link below to register to that same webinar that will change your life:

That link again:

www.robertsmallbone.com

AUTHOR BIOS

Robert Smallbone started his internet marketing career in 2015 and is also the co-owner of 2 real property companies based in the UK. With a vision of helping 1,000,000,000 people through education, he will be making a BIG name for himself in years to come. So, watch this space.

Connect with him on Facebook at:

www.facebook.com/robertsmallbonepublicfigure

Alternatively connect with him on Twitter at:

twitter.com/SmallboneRobert

Or Instagram at:

www.instagram.com/robert_smallbone_1988

Visit his e-book store at:

www.achieveanythingandeverything.com

See you on the other side!

TABLE OF CONTENTS

Chapter 1: Introduction

    Foreword……………………………….... 9
    History of Sales and Marketing…………… 10
    Factors Affecting Sales Volume………….. 12
    Why Many Businesses Fail at
    Selling Products & Services……………….. 16
    How this eBook Resolves the Problem…… 17

Chapter 2: Important Concepts………………………………………19

    Marketing versus Public Relations………... 20
    Products and Services……………………... 21
    Target Market……………………………… 21
    Niche Market and Niche Marketing……..... 22
    Branding…………………………………… 22
    Leads and Conversions……………………..23
    Search Engine Optimization………………..24
    Internal and External Customers……………25
    Affiliate Marketing………………………… 26

Key Influencers..................................27

Chapter 3: Before Getting Started.................. 29

Market Research..............................… 30
Market Personas...............................… 31
Business Plan.................................. 32
Mission & Vision............................... 34
SMART Goals................................... 35

Chapter 4: 50 Ways to Increase Your Sales........ 37

25 Online Marketing Tips to Boost Sales….. 38
15 Networking & Relationship-Building Tips to Boost Sales…................................ 67
5 Audio-visual Tips to Boost Sales............82
3 Print Media Tips to Boost Sales............. 87
2 Product or Service Tips to Boost Sales…... 90

Conclusion.. 93

INTRODUCTION

FOREWORD

In today's marketplace, getting ahead of the competition can feel like running 200 mph on a hamster wheel. It's hard to distinguish your brand from the noise of everyone else's, especially from the top dogs in the industry who've been around longer and have the resources to shout louder than everyone else.

Many big brands are also owned by **bigger** brands, providing them with inexhaustible funds for hiring celebrities, promoting on every possible medium, and pulling big PR stunts. Even so, small and medium sized businesses have plenty of ways to carve out their own niche in the market.

This is because these businesses tend to have something bigger companies don't have: a more selectively targeted audience. Smaller and medium sized businesses also have better opportunities to build a rapport with customers and learn who they are, what they want, and how to get it to them.

This marketing edge helps many small and medium sized businesses to thrive by homing in on their niche and tailoring their marketing plans, products, and services, to meet their specific needs. But how?

In this new book, the aim is to answer this question with 50 easy-to-use tips for entrepreneurs looking to make big sales on a small budget. But first, let's take a look at the history of sales and marketing, how they have transformed over the years, and what you can expect to encounter in the field today.

HISTORY OF SALES AND MARKETING

Sales and marketing have always been intertwined. Even in eras and cultures where bartering played a huge role in commerce, the two parties had to effectively market their goods to make a "sale" by convincing the buyer of its worth. After all, why take two mangoes for one apple when you can convince the buyer that it's worth four? It's all in the sales pitch.

The sales pitch, however, only represents a small scale and individualistic approach to marketing, from one seller to a potential buyer. This changed in the mid-1400s when the printing press gave rise to the mass-production of brochures, fliers, and pamphlets.

Then in the 1700s the first magazine was born, and in the 1800s, the first billboard.

As industrialization and capitalism took the world by storm, sales and marketing became even more important. Business owners now had to compete amongst themselves on a large scale to reach customers all around the world. By the late 1900s, marketing took another leap when computers gave birth to digital marketing,0 and then in the 2000s a more integrated and complex form of marketing took root.

In the digital age, pamphlets, fliers, and even business cards have become less important as most consumers get information about products and services through digital means. Because of this, the 2010s saw an exponential growth in companies moving into social media and other online spaces to build connections with customers in hopes of converting that engagement into sales.

And you know what? It's been working!

FACTORS AFFECTING SALES VOLUME

To better understand how to improve sales, entrepreneurs must first understand what affects the volume of sales. There are, of course, many contributing factors, and this can differ based on the industry, the disposable income of the target market, and how consumers may react to price changes.

More general factors affecting sales volume, regardless of industry and the target market, are the level of competition, the size of the business making the sales, the price of the goods, and the talent of the workforce behind the company. Let us examine each of these in detail.

Competition

Competition refers to the threat of another business proving to your target market that anything you can do, they can do better, provide more value while doing it, and maybe even do so more quickly and at a lower price. The more unrestricted a market is, then the stiffer the competition. Competition may at first seem like a bad thing, but through competition companies innovate, grow, and find more efficient ways to do business.

The most obvious form of competition is when businesses create similar products and begin to squabble for their share of the target market. This might include two soda companies, or three restaurants on the same block. However, another form of competition many entrepreneurs overlook occurs when your target market begins to substitute the goods you make with something you don't.

For instance, if you own a company that specializes in making and selling pasta, the most obvious contenders are other brands of pasta. But there are other competitors as well. There's the convenience of simply eating out at the Italian restaurant up the street. Why not pizza instead of pasta? Why not a salad? And what if your customers pick up a new fad and join a no-carb liquid-diet this week, so they buy kale and fruit instead?

Because of this, brands must expand their thinking when it comes to competition. This helps them craft better sales pitches, and better ads, to convince customers they are the best alternative among all the others.

Business Size

Big businesses tend to enjoy bigger inventories, and therefore bigger sales potential. This increases the opportunity to make a profit. As previously mentioned, bigger businesses also have deeper pockets to dip into when it's time to promote products, or call in big PR favors. The sheer volume of sales these companies make often turn into a form of marketing in and of itself. The more customers see a particular product, the more they trust it and buy it.

Also mentioned was that smaller companies can embrace another form of marketing these behemoths cannot. They can form, and capitalize on, intimate relationships with customers to boost sales. This helps to grow and stabilize sales volume via customer loyalty. Think about it. Who do you think knows their friends and fans best? The company with 10, or the one with 10,000?

Price

One of the most common ways businesses compete with each other is to sell at the lowest price possible without sacrificing a profit. Again, the bigger a company, the more capable they are of doing so. The higher the volume of output at the factories, and the higher the volume of sales, the lower the cost of production over time.

In academic business circles, this is called "economy of scale."

Other companies may choose to take a different route by keeping their goods pricey to match the value (real or perceived) of their product. High prices also make goods more exclusive, since not very many people in the market can afford them. If the company makes only a few of these item, then even better! One company who does this to their benefit is Bentley.

Workforce Talent

An often underrated factor affecting sales, many marketers and public relations specialist often forget to team up with human resources to improve workforce talent. How do the skills and abilities of the workforce behind a company affect sales? Let us consider this example.

Have you ever needed to buy a technical product you know nothing about? Maybe a new laptop, a Wi-Fi router, or a professional camera? You know two stores and decide to try them both. In Store 1, a worker notices your struggle and comes by to help you make a selection. He makes suggestions and explains the pros and cons of each. Even at checkout, the cashier commends you on the choice you made while you're waiting in line.

At Store 2, no one approaches to help you. You ask one guy in the company shirt wandering around the aisles if he can help, but he looks twice as confused as you. While you're waiting in the checkout line, hoping you got the right product, the cashier comments, "I didn't even know we sold these here. What's that???" Who would you buy from?

WHY MANY BUSINESSES FAIL AT SELLING PRODUCTS & SERVICES

In spite of the wealth of knowledge available about sales and marketing, many businesses still fail miserably at selling their products and services. Because of this, 80% of startups fail within a year. Having considered the general factors affecting sales, what are some of the more specific reasons some products and services become lost in the noise?

I've put together a list.

- Lack of planning
- Poor leadership
- Poor customer relations
- Too little or too much inventory

- Failure to differentiate the product or service
- Refusal to innovate
- Not reinvesting profits into the business
- Failing to invest in employees

HOW THIS EBOOK RESOLVES THE PROBLEM

This new eBook boosts your sales by providing 50 tips for tackling many of the problems businesses face that affect sales volumes and inventory turnover rates. To do this, I have done a lot more than throw together a "listicle" with 50 tips. Instead, I have provided sufficient background information, explained key terms, and even threw in five bonus tips to help you get started.

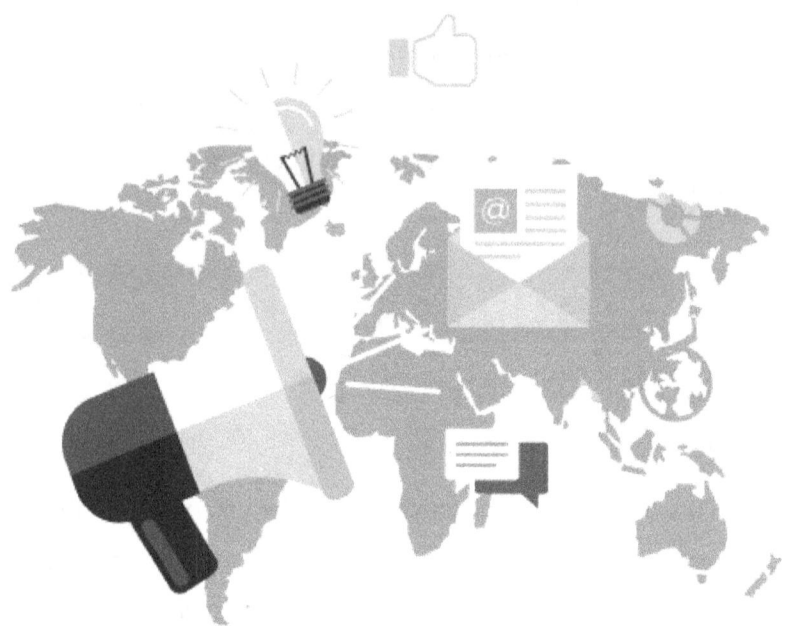

Unlike many other sales and marketing guides, the aim of this is to keep the language simple and the tips easy to follow. Throughout the book, I also suggest tried and true methods that I have used and that I have learnt from my mentors that help to boost sales and inventory turnover rates in our businesses, and I am confident that you can use them to do the same.

IMPORTANT CONCEPTS

To further simplify the learning process in this book, here are some important concepts you should become familiar with. They'll makes it easier to follow the information ahead, and to understand other marketing material available to you, should you choose to expand your research.

MARKETING VERSUS PUBLIC RELATIONS

In the past there were more distinct differences between marketing and public relations. Both fields tackled different tasks. Marketing aimed to boost sales by making the brand and all its products and services as visible to the public as possible.

Public relations, on the other hand, mostly focused on building and managing relationships, directing crisis communications, and securing media opportunities.

Today, as public relations moves into a more digital era and integrates with marketing, the tools are shared. Both fields work on ads, manage social media, practice SEO, and understand that "content is king." However, the overall goals have not changed. Marketing is still more focused on growing sales through being seen; and public relations, through building a connection and loyalty with customers.

PRODUCTS AND SERVICES

Every company produces goods of some sort. "Goods" may refer to either products or services. Products are tangible items made by the company for its customers. Services are intangible goods, including technology, provided to meet the needs and wants of customers, or to solve problems.

TARGET MARKET

Many companies simply want to target everyone. After all, the more people you reach, the better, right? On the surface, this seems sensible, but it can lead to big budget spending without the matching results. The better approach is to know your audience, and to home in on a particular group known as the target market.

Your target market should embody the characteristics of the ideal customer, or the people most likely to buy your goods and services. Keep in mind that these characteristics may change over time and that the customers you do attract might not even be the ones you originally intended to.

Need an example? Consider Viagra, and how what initially started out as heart medication later become infinitely better known for its distinctive side effect.

NICHE MARKET AND NICHE MARKETING

BRANDING

Even more specific than a target market is a niche market. While "target market" generally refers to the group of people a business wants to turn into customers, niche marketing refers to tailoring products and services to entice a specific small and specialized demographic in the population. These groups are usually small internal elements of larger groups. Examples of niches include retro gamers, vegans who eat organically and gluten-free, and high-end car enthusiasts.

Branding refers to a deliberate effort to market goods and services in a particular way to potential and existing customers. This may include obvious things like logo, appearance, and affiliations. More subtle forms of branding may look at what descriptions go best with the brand, who uses it, and how best to associate it with a particular group or niche.

LEADS AND CONVERSIONS

Leads refer to potential customers of a product or service. When a consumer shows interest in a product and begins to do research, or visits the company website or store, they are leads. A consumer is also still a lead, though a more promising one, if they choose to accept a free sample or free trial of your products and services. Leads become conversions when the initial interest results in a sale.

SEARCH ENGINE OPTIMIZATION

Search engine optimization (SEO) is the process of making content more discoverable online by engaging in practices that increase page rankings in search engines. Ideally, most companies hope to show up on the first page as the answer to questions users ask, or the solution to their problems. Depending on the industry, some may also wish to appear as experts in a certain area, or to provide entertainment.

WebFire 3.0 is a great software that automatically grabs free traffic and leads that you can cash in on for any niche. Watch the demonstration video below by clicking on the link.

http://www.webfire.com/a/?id=33430&p=1

INTERNAL AND EXTERNAL CUSTOMERS

When most people think of customers, they think of people directly purchasing the goods they offer. However, these are only external customers. Internal customers refer to the workforce behind the company. Smart entrepreneurs ensure they build great relationships with both. A happy employee, especially in the sales and customer service areas, often translates into satisfied customers.

It is vital to build a relationship with a database of people. Adding customers to an e-mail database is essential for online success. Imagine the power of being able to send an e-mail out to your list of 10,000 + people, knowing that they are hungry to buy. On average, every customer on an e-mail list is worth $1 per month.

So a list of 10,000 people should on average generate a business $10,000 per month. Of course, it is not all about selling. It is important to provide great content and value to your database as well as selling. It takes between 5-7 interactions with a customer online before they will purchase.

Get Response and Aweber are both very useful tools for building an online database for your business. Get Response also offers a free training program too online. Click below to find out more about Get Reponse.

http://www.getresponse.com/index/robbo1988

And Aweber

http://aweber.com/?469561

They both do the same things so you will not need both. Just one or the other. Whichever you prefer the user interface for.

AFFILIATE MARKETING

Since sales make or break a business, taking the task on alone can prove daunting. To help make this easier, many companies share the work with key influencers willing to help promote their products and service. In this setup, other people and businesses help to market the product and send traffic (or leads) to the website or the online store via unique hyperlinks.

Some companies pay for the traffic and others for actual purchases. In turn, they provide their brand ambassadors with a commission per sale. In some instances, the company may provide free products instead, or in addition to commissions.

Click Funnels (more on them later) offer the chance to win a car through their affiliate program. Find out more at:

KEY INFLUENCERS

http://tiny.cc/d6r3gy

Key influencers and industry experts have a lot in common. People respect their position in their respective fields, and any brand associated with them often benefits from the relationship. But while experts typically offer technical know-how related to the industry, key influencers offer popularity and their position as cultural icons.

For instance, an actor or famous musician are key influencers in an industry, but probably know very little about how to film and edit a movie, or how to record and produce music. Likewise, a football athlete may be a star quarterback on the field, but know very little about how the helmet protecting his head is made, or where his shoes came from.

Even so, associating the athlete with your brand of helmet or shoes brings in a lot of great PR for you, because he is a key influencer.

BEFORE GETTING STARTED

Now that you understand the background behind sales and marketing, and all the key concepts, it may seem like time to jump into the meat of the matter. However, there are still a few things entrepreneurs need to do before getting started. These are so essential that you might as well consider them an extra five tips on how to boost your sales.

One of the most important steps entrepreneurs should take before starting a business is to do market research. This comes even before working on a business plan, or seeking out investment capital. But why? The answer is simple: market research tells you if this is even a business idea worth pursuing in the first place.

MARKET RESEARCH

Market research may involve a full study and/or the use of surveys. If you already jumped the gun and got the business started, you can also use services like WebFire to find out who your customers are, and get information on competitors.

Good market research provides the following information:

- A proper analysis of the industry, and whether or not it's worth entering
- The feasibility of the business idea within the overall industry
- The competitors within the industry
- What competitors lack that you can provide
- The target or niche market

- A proposed strategy for reaching the target market
- Expected or projected sales, revenue, profits

MARKET PERSONAS

Entrepreneurs can use the information provided by market research to further understand and describe their target markets via market personas. Market personas, sometimes called buyer personas, are fictional "characters" describing the ideal or generalized representation of the customer base.

When making market personas, some of the information companies may try to include for the fictional profiles include:

- Profession
- Level of education
- Age
- Gender or sex
- Ethnicity
- Salary or disposable income
- Location
- Family or household size
- Hobbies and personal interests

Market personas are an integral part of upping your marketing game plan because it helps you to intimately understand the inner workings of your target market. For instance, when creating an ad, you now know what profession to use in the plot, how old the actors should be, what gender or sex, and how much diversity to include.

You also know if promotional pieces with single or family households will work better, and what hobbies may appeal to the demographic.

BUSINESS PLANS

Like market research, a business plan is one of the most underrated tools for success in the business world. Some entrepreneurs swear by them, while many others insist they're a waste of time. Our verdict? Better to have even a brief one than none at all. Here's why: a business plan is exactly that, a plan for your business. There's an old saying, "If you fail to plan, you plan to fail."

Writing a business plan forces entrepreneurs to be proactive and make key decisions before problems arise. In businesses based on partnerships, signing off on the business plan can prevent disagreements later on. And of course, business plans help to secure loans and other investments as it provides something concrete for investors to look at, especially for businesses not yet in operation.

Some of the key areas business plans compel entrepreneurs to make decisions on include:

- Mission and vision
- Management
- Target market
- Product and services offerings
- Competition
- Research, design, and development
- Market Plan
- Operations and management
- Personnel plan
- Risk and identification management
- Financial overview
- Sales forecast
- Profit and loss statement (projected, or real)
- Balance Sheet (projected, or real)

For an in depth book on business planning, Alice Graham's 'Planning Your Business Success' provides key information on how to goal set and much more.

http://www.achieveanythingandeverything.com/bookshare.html?bookId=207463

MISSION AND VISION

Mentioned above in the list of things entrepreneurs iron out in business plans, mission and vision statements play an important role in business. A mission statement defines the purpose of the organization in terms of what it does, how it is does it or why, and who the customers are. The vision statement puts into words what the company hopes to achieve and where it sees itself in the not-so-distant future.

Mission and vision statements are important because they set the tone for the rest of the organization, and for business operations. It also speaks to what the company values above everything else, making it easier to prioritize tasks and resources accordingly. Finally, it provides direction to new partners, investors, and employees who need to be reminded of why the company does what it does, and where it's headed.

SMART GOALS

Most mission and vision statements only briefly sum up a company's goals and objectives, but when doing business, companies need SMART goals to work towards, especially as it relates to sales, profit, and visibility. But what are SMART goals? SMART goals are those that are specific, measurable, achievable, relevant, and time bound.

For example, one SMART goal in sales would be: *To improve the sale of Product X by 25%by the next financial quarter.*

A not so SMART goal in sales would be: *To start improving sales by the end of the week.*

50 WAYS TO INCREASE YOUR SALES

In today's market, sales make or break a company. After all, if no one buys a product or service then the company has no revenue to cover expenses, and no way to make a profit. By increasing sales volumes, companies are able to stay ahead of the competition and invest in growing the business further.

25 ONLINE MARKETING TIPS TO BOOST SALES

Here are 50 ways to increase your sales today!

As more people move into digital spaces to hang out, share updates, and obtain information, many brands follow suit. This helps companies to connect with potential and existing customers on platforms that are most convenient to buyers. It also helps to build relationships in a more relaxed environment where consumers are not necessarily pressured to purchase anything.

Another great benefit of online marketing is that most online marketing options start off free. It doesn't cost a dime to make a Twitter, Instagram, or Pinterest account. Of course there are great companies out there that can simplify the process and make it easier to manage multiple accounts, but at the most basic level, online marketing is 100% free. Here's how to make it work for you.

Marketing Tip 1: Build a Website

As people become more computer and internet literate, virtually everyone has a website, and so should you. Having a website can help to legitimize your business. It can also make the company and its products and services more likely to pop up in searches online.

In addition to this, websites act as a central hub, providing information
customers might otherwise have a difficult time getting on their own. By answering these questions, companies reduce uncertainty and increase the likelihood of a purchase. It's also a great place to add social media links so potential customers can keep in touch. Many companies also add their online stores to their websites.

There are easy ways to build websites on platforms like WordPress.org. However, if you fail to use the right platform for hosting, the website may run slowly and crash frequently.

To prevent this from happening research hosting companies using Google. Most services are user-friendly, easy to upgrade, offer unlimited storage, and provide excellent awesome 24/7 support team.

How to Get Started

There are many different web hosts out there. Finding the one that caters to your specific needs is easier than you may think. With Websites like Webs And Wix, the task of starting a beautiful website has never been so easy. With their drag and drop platforms, you can have a website complete with all the bells and whistles in the space of just one day. They also have great annual starter plans to get you started.

Wix is a recommended website builder and you can build your website for free. Click on the links below to get started.

http://wixstats.com/?a=9941&c=124&s1=

http://wixstats.com/?a=9941&c=2252&s1=

Marketing Tip 2: Create an Online Store

As more people consume information and make purchases online, not having an online store is likely to cost you a lot of money. By building an online store, even local businesses with one physical store in the middle of nowhere can make ten times the sales all around the world. Customers nearby will also appreciate the ease of making their orders online.

Online stores also provide free advertising, and once again help companies to rank highly when potential customers look for goods to meet their needs. Alongside an online store attached to a website, companies can consider using major platforms like Facebook, Amazon, and eBay.

How to Start

Most Web servers offer hosting for online stores. If you are not HTML savvy, your webmaster can get this going for you. All it takes is a little know how. The important thing to remember is to be clear. The structure of your store should be defined and to the point with all links going directly down the sales funnel.

Many web stores these days have links that do not take you where you thought you were going. Your call-to-action buttons should also look like exactly what they are. There is nothing that will drive a potential customer away faster than a web store that is hard to use.

Marketing Tip 3: Make Online Purchases Easy

Being able to order products and services online is one of the greatest conveniences of the modern era. Even restaurants like Pizza Hut let customers order online and either deliver it to their door or let them pick it up at the store. Yet many online stores struggle with making sales.

Why? Because the checkout section is complicated and full of distractions.
Eliminate all the bells, whistles, and hoops to jump through at checkout. Don't force customers to create accounts, or restrict payment options. And try not to run ads on that page. Your competitor just might run off with your customers by showing them a better option.

Where to Focus Your Attention

Make the checkout process smooth by exercising restraint when it comes to things like "Customers who bought this item also liked..." and related strategies. A clean visual approach and no distractions cuts down on hemming and hawing, and the possibility of a changed mind and an abandoned purchase, on the buyer's part.

Try offering packages as an alternative to attempting to chain purchases together. Bundling related products and offering a discount on the combined purchase incentivizes customers to explore your full catalog. A good example is Adobe, which bundles its pdf readers and editors in its software store.

Marketing Tip 4: Add Your Business to Maps

An online store is great, but a brick and mortar building still has its purposes. How? The building itself provides free marketing 24/7, especially if it faces a main street. But more importantly, you can add a brick and mortar building to Google maps. This makes your business more likely to come up in local searches. This is especially important for businesses that can only offer services locally, such as carpenters, plumbers, and caterers.

If you work from home, then this is still an option. Simply use the address of your home office. For companies providing services, people are more likely to call than show up anyway. Be sure to add your number and other important contact information to make you easy to reach, along with a link to your website.

Often times, Google may ask for pictures of the work site. You can instead use these pictures to showcase your work whether it's delicious dishes, beautiful hardwood floors, or a great paint job.

Where To Go To Get Started

To make use of the Google business site, you will need to start a business account. Here Google will let you enter all your information and they will automatically add you to Google maps, with space for adding custom photos during the registration process. This service is completely free, as in exchange Google gets to remain current on business listings. You can't beat free, which takes us to our next tip.

Marketing Tip 5: Give Away Stuff for Free

Giving away free stuff sounds like a great way to lose money, not increase sales, but you can use free goodies to rope customers in. This is why many apps and software companies allow trial versions that are restricted, only last for a certain period of time, or both. Big companies like Microsoft and Spotify do this all the time, and it's a great strategy for smaller businesses who can afford to do the same.

If you're not able to give stuff away on a large scale, then consider giving away free samples to key influencers in return for an honest review. With the right incentives, many of these people may also become brand ambassadors and help to push your brand to their audience. They can also do this through affiliate marketing.

Click funnels is a brilliant platform that allows you to create a sales funnel. This means that you can give away a free product or service and then lead customers down a funnel. This means that they can then be given the opportunity to buy a small priced product (i.e. $37) then a higher priced product (i.e $197) and so on.

Once set up this funnel is automatic and you also can have e-mails automatically linked in to the funnel so that you can build a database of customers at the same time.

Click on the link below to get a 14-day free trial for Click Funnels

http://tiny.cc/ryr3gy

Example

In Covington Georgia, a roadside vendor offered "free" homemade wine. The wine was free, it turned out, only if you bought a lemon for five dollars. That is an example of how the word "free" brings people running. When you print the word "free," you get everyone's attention. Offer the free item, then while they are there, you can give them your specials on the items you are selling.

Do not be too pushy, as that can make customers take the free item and leave your site. Instead make the offers too good to pass up and let them speak for themselves. 90% of the time, customers will want to hear more if a deal is enticing enough.

Marketing Tip 6: Offer Only One Product or Service on the Home Page

This may seem counterintuitive, especially for companies with multiple offerings across a wide range, but trying to sell too many things on the landing page makes for bad website copy, and it's too aggressive a sales pitch. Offering just one product on the home page keeps things simple and creates focus. Interested customers will usually check out the rest of the products for themselves anyway.

Why This Is Vital

Take the old saying, "slow and steady wins the race," to heart. When you overwhelm the potential customer, they go into a state of panic. When that happens, they get confused and have to back out and go somewhere else. That is not what you want, because it is your competitors they are going to seek out next time. One deal on the landing page is good enough to get them looking for more.

Start with the best deal you have and show them their savings. When they see that, they will go find some more deals that will save them money. It is also good to add savings to all your listings. People these days want to know what the regular price is and how it compares to the sale.

Marketing Tip 7: Offer Fewer Choices in General

The best way to boost sales is to offer something for everyone, right? The obvious answer might seem like a "yes" but experts show that the more decisions you offer prospective customers, the more indecision you create.

The more indecision a potential customer grapples with, the more your offerings seem complicated and risky, and the greater their sense of unease. To reduce the likelihood of this, focus on your best strengths, or consolidate similar offerings into one.

A Perfect Example

On Amazon they offer just the right number of choices without going too far. People are fearful of making the wrong choice, so when faced with a barrage of choices they will often times back out and go somewhere else. Some people are not capable of making tough decisions.

Determine which services and goods are performing best, then list those services prominently and prune other options away from listing pages. This has the added benefit of highlighting your best sellers, and interested customers will browse less popular items on their own time.

Marketing Tip 8: Use Ad Extensions to Increase Clicks

Available on both AdWords and Bing, this extension makes ads bigger and provides more places for potential customers to click. The amazing part is that it doesn't cost a dime extra to set up this feature, and it naturally increases the click rate. Ad extensions can showcase more product offerings, contact information, and even the rating your store or company received from customers. The choice is yours.

Where Do You Go to Set This Feature Up?

When you go to Google Adwords, you will have to use your Google account sign in. If you do not have a Google account, you can start one for free. By adding this feature not only will you add clickable options, but you will also get paid for every time someone clicks on the link. Does this option have your attention yet?

Google Adwords also offers agreements in which all traffic generates profit. Even visitors who don't make purchases still count as clicks, and thus as money in your pocket. Pay-per-click was introduced in the late 90's and has become a trend these days. You get paid for doing nothing at all. Many businesses have jumped on the PPC train as a way to generate additional revenue using site space as rental real estate.

Marketing Tip 9: Use High Quality Pictures

Another way to improve ads and increase clicks and conversions is by using high quality photos. There are many free stock photo options online where professional photographers donate pieces to the public domain to build exposure. However, for more unique photos, companies should consider buying the rights to premium images on sites like Shutterstock.

Another great option is to take the pictures yourself, especially if these are pictures of the actual product. Keep the photos professional, with great lighting, and from all possible angles. This may seem like overkill, but customers like to know what they're getting themselves into before making it to check out.

Marketing Tip 10: Use Relevant Landing Pages

There's nothing more annoying than clicking on an ad about a particular thing only to be taken to a page that has nothing to do with the proposed offer. Choose a landing page for your ad that is directly relevant to the promoted content.

For instance, if you're promoting a particular 10% off deal online, then the landing page should provide details on that specific deal, and the option to make a purchase. It should not take customers to the home page or a Twitter account.

Lead Pages is a useful tool for building relevant landing pages. You can customize, A/B Split test and create multiple landing pages for multiple products/services that you wish to market.

http://link.leadpages.net/aff_c?offer_id=6&aff_id=20836

Examples of Clickbait

Clickbait articles usually start with titles like "You have just won a free laptop!" How did it feel when you clicked on that one for the first time only to find that the link went to an online survey? I bet you never clicked on one of those again, did you? Chances are you felt like everyone else did when I fell for that one: hoodwinked and cheated.

The same applies to your links. There is nothing more annoying than clicking on a link marked "apples" and ending up on a page about "oranges." Relevance is the key to getting returning online traffic.

Marketing Tip 11: Add Opt-In Pop-Ups

In all honesty, this can be really annoying for the casual browser just looking for information. But if people really love your products and services, they will want to opt-in for special offerings and information. It's a great way to build an email list, but try not to spam customers. Provide information on the best deals, discounts, general information, or well-wishes for the upcoming holiday seasons.

Even with a plan in place, managing email lists can become tricky, especially if it requires being available on or right before major holidays to write great copy for customers. Companies like Aweber can help to make the process easier by allowing you to send automated emails on beautiful templates with reliable deliverability and the ability to track how the emails perform via a mobile app.

How To Add An Alert To Your Website

The best way to add a pop-up is to incorporate code into your index page. It has to be in the form of javascript in order for it to work like you want it. Here's a small piece of code you could add in between your <head> and </head> tags in your html code.

```
<script language="Javascript">
<!--
alert ("Alert Message")
//-->
</script>
```

All you will have to do is change the words in red to whatever message you are trying to get across to the visitor. You can add something like: "Did you know that we are selling all shoes at

20% off the normal price!" If you are not familiar with HTML then your webmaster can do this for you.

Marketing Tip 12: Optimize for Mobile Browsing and Purchases

Back in 2015, Google announced that most people now browse online via smartphones. Many internet users also make purchases via their phones, whether via websites or apps. To make the best of this, brands must ensure that the websites are optimized for mobile use. This means keeping content concise, using simple designs, using icons instead of text wherever possible, and making the website as fast as possible.

Try not to force users to download an app in order to use a mobile friendly version of your website. This takes time, megabytes, and costs users space on their phones. Some may also be wary of installing apps from companies they never heard of before.

How Is This Done?

You will need to create a mobile duplicate or adaptation of your regular website, which you can do via Android's App Inventor and related brand-specific sites and services. Once the mobile site is functional, provide a clear link to it from your landing page.

Marketing Tip 13: Offer a Solid Money-Back Guarantee

While words, in the form of testimonials and product specifications, provide a great opportunity to build trust, actions always speak louder than words. When companies put their money where their mouths are with promises like "if you're not satisfied, we'll issue a full refund!" customers listen. This eases any fears the customers may have about needing to return the product if they are dissatisfied with it, and thus increases the likelihood of a purchase.

Marketing Tip 14: Make a Purchase Seem Urgent

There's a reason many sales pitches mention phrases like "for a limited time only" and "this one-time offer." Some companies even up the sense of urgency by using counters to illustrate that time is running out before the sale or the item's availability ends.

This sense of urgency tells customers that they need to make a quick decision now or risk missing out on a great deal forever. The need to make a quick decision can easily double or triple sales through impulsive buys. The longer a customer tends to think over a purchase, the less likely they are to go through with it as other offers and expenses pop up.

Another way to push the sense of urgency is through your mailing list. If you do a three-day deal, for instance, you can email your list once on the first day. This will bring in some sales. On the second day, you'd email them twice. This won't bring in a ton of sales either, but you should see some growth in sales.

But then the third day, you'd e-mail them three times – once in the morning; once in the afternoon, warning that the deal is about to end; and once in the evening, saying there's only a few hours left. On the final mailings, you should see sales grow exponentially, especially in the final minutes leading up to the deadline.

Marketing Tip 15: Encourage Users to Buy in Bulk

Another direct way of improving sales is by encouraging customers to buy in bulk. To do this, you must make the bulk price cheaper than the price of a single item. For instance, why buy just one shirt for $10 when you can buy two shirts for $18 or three for $25? Ensure that the prices for bulk are low enough to encourage customers to make larger purchases, but high enough to ensure the company still makes a good profit.

Marketing Tip 16: Make Detailed FAQs

At the onset of starting up a business or running an online store, finding resources to dedicate to customer service can be a real challenge. To work around this, make a detailed FAQ so that customers can get the answers they need without long wait times, dealing with confusing operators, or waiting for responses to emails and social media queries.

FAQs should cover all possible questions customers may ask about the product or service. Don't assume any question is too silly. Keep updating the FAQs as the questions role in via phone call, social media, in person, or any other medium.

Making an FAQ

Record the questions people ask frequently. Make a FAQ page and list the questions along with their answers. A good example would be:

Q: How do you stay in business with your prices so low?

A: By quantity and quality. We know if we sell you a quality product, you will be back for more.

Create a link on your homepage marked "FAQ." Not only will this inform the asker that you are all about good customer service, but you will have their question answered before they ask it. Also, have a contact form at the bottom of the FAQ page for them to ask a question that is not listed. This will let them know that you are willing to answer any questions that they may have.

Marketing Tip 17: Focus on the Product, Not the Company

One of the key mistakes companies make when marketing products is to focus on the company a tad too much. At first glance, it might seem like the best approach. Why not talk up the company? That's great for branding, and it gets the word out there about how amazing the company is.

However, customers generally aren't concerned about the company. Most customers purchase something to fill a need, satisfy a desire, or to solve a problem. They want to know how the shirt, software, or meal can meet their needs. The company behind the product itself isn't nearly as important, and if they need that information, well… that's what an 'About Us' page is for.

Marketing Tip 18: Copy the Customer's Voice

Write engaging copy! That's the most common advice you hear for online marketing, but what's engaging to one person is downright boring to someone else. So how do you write engaging content for your customer base? Simple. With market research, you can learn about your target market and market personas help to narrow it all down.

Once you know who the target market is, then it's time to understand how they speak, what they love, and what their value systems are. The more you sound like your customer base and echo **their** values, the more customers can relate to not just the copy, but the product and the brand.

Unless you're a seasoned writer with a master's in English this can seem like a huge task to take on. To make you a more confident writer, consider taking courses at a local university, or online. This helps you learn how to write for an online audience, as this is much different from writing for other groups.

Marketing Tip 19: Build Social Media Presence

One of the easiest ways to build online presence is with social media. Even professionals and brands with no websites use social media platforms like Twitter, Facebook, LinkedIn, and Google Plus. Social media also represents the hangout hub for most millennials, making it the best place to find and interact with customers.

To boost social media presence, try automating posts through services like WebFire. This makes it easier to set up posts to run for days, weeks, or months in advance, without needing to be online all day every day to maintain a social media presence.

Another great piece of software is Social Oomph. Social Oomph enables you to set up auto respond messages that automatically send message to people that follow you on twitter or friend you on Facebook.

http://www.socialoomph.com/98559.html

Interacting with customers is one of the key ways entrepreneurs can use social media to increase sales. Look for posts about problems your products can fix and provide the solution. If a customer posts a great comment about your product or service, thank them. If a customer posts a not-so-great comment, apologize and make an effort to resolve the issue immediately. A great customer service experience can do wonders to make amends.

There are some great courses out there that provide quality training on how to utilize Facebook Ads to generate leads and sales for your business. Click on the link below to learn more.

https://goo.gl/Vm1GMc

Marketing Tip 20: Utilize Search Engine Optimization

As mentioned earlier, search engine optimization helps companies to rank higher in search engine results. But how? There are many ways to make this possible.

Some people stuff the content on their web pages and blogs with keywords people are most likely to search for online. Others may sneak keywords into saved pictures, infographics, and even the HTML code in the backend of the website or webpage. One service that helps customers to boost rankings quickly is WebFire. The company does this in a number of ways, such as:

- Providing free exposure by ensuring you rank on the first page of Google, Yahoo, and Bing.
- Tracking high traffic keywords for use in your content.
- Helping you to purchase high-ranking domains for a fraction of the original value.

http://www.webfire.com/a/?id=33430&p=1

Recently, however, brands have been moving away from overusing keywords and have begun trying to make content so inspiring and interesting that people feel compelled to share it. This means not just great blog posts, but also great audio-visual productions.

Marketing Tip 21: Publish Press Releases

A staple of public relations, press releases are just as important today as they were ten years ago. However, much has changed in how they're created and published. Many companies tend to get creative with press releases via interviews, video announcements, newsletters, and even social media posts.

No matter how creative a company gets with their press release however, if no one sees a release, no one gets the opportunity to appreciate it. Companies like WebFire can help you to distribute that press release to a wider audience all across the internet.

http://www.webfire.com/a/?id=33430&p=1

The Best Way to Get the Press to Open and Read Your E-mail

Let's face it, the whole trick is to get the press to read your statement. If the subject is not engaging, then your press release will be marked as spam and all future releases condemned along with it. Engaging subject lines speak directly to the target audience, playing on their interests and hobbies to drive up interest. Once the reader opens the email, use strategies like video content, sharp photography, and humor to ensure that they read your release with interest.

Marketing Tip 23: Use a Tier Pricing Strategy

Have you ever noticed that most software companies and service providers offer many different packages? These packages may range from free to standard to premium. They may also be called platinum, gold, silver, and bronze. Each category then reflects a particular price and set of matching perks.

Studies show that most customers will choose the middle offer, and so companies should focus more intensely on that offer in terms of price, offerings, and even marketing. A price tier strategy also helps to improve sales by ensuring that there's something for everyone. It also provides you with the opportunity to offer an upgrade later on.

Marketing Tip 24: Utilize Call to Action

Today's consumers are bombarded left and right with information and ads from organizations all over the world. In response, consumers have become adept at ignoring most obvious sales pitches. They skim through pages to get the information they need, and then move on.

Even so, a good call to action incorporated with great content can turn leads into conversions. It's that last push customers need to make that final decision. Calls to action can be incorporated into your independent website, as well as into social media pages like Instagram and Facebook. They can also be used alongside ads.

Some businesses may use options like "Learn More" or "Contact Us", while some go for hard sells like "Buy Now" or "Add to Cart".

Marketing Tip 25: Track and Analyze Data

One of the big mistakes companies make, especially when the current marketing plan is doing just fine, is to never track or analyze their data. You might think if things are working fine, then why bother? The answer is an easy one: because it can help you save money. Imagine throwing money at several different avenues, but only three of them are actually bringing in customers. Why spend money – or as much money – on the others?

Another reason data analytics are important is so that companies can create a mission and vision and craft SMART goals to help them get there. How do you know where you want to be if you don't quite know where you are now?

Analytics help to paint a more accurate picture of the current sales and marketing situation, and to show trends. This can help you make more informed decisions about the way forward.

Doing this work manually can be incredibly time consuming, so to make it easier, you should consider using applications built for this exact purpose. Companies can help track important data like:

- Inventory turnover rate
- Conversion rate
- Social media reach
- Customer ratings and complaints
- Most popular keywords
- Customer demographics

The Best Data Analysis for Your Dollar

Google offers a free service, Google analytics, that will track your traffic and content. They give you a small snippet of code to put right after the opening body tag of your home page. The code looks like this:

```
<?php include_once("analyticstracking.php") ?>
```

Adding this code will link your website to your Google analytics account, which allows you to track all kinds of pertinent statistics. These include sales, traffic, and link information. This is a must have for any company with an online store.

15 NETWORKING & RELATIONSHIP BUILDING TIPS TO BOOST SALES

When it comes to sales and marketing, an often overlooked method of boosting sales volumes is through networking and relationship-building. This is where public relations practices step in to fill the gap, and produce results. Networking and building relationships take time, but every connection is another opportunity for growth and exposure.

By building relationships with internal and external customers, industry leaders, key influencers, and the general public, companies stand a much better chance of taking giant steps forward ahead of the competition. Here are 15 ways you can harness industry connections and great relationships to start boosting sales.

Marketing Tip 26: Work on Social Skills

Have you ever noticed how hard it is to say no to a well dressed and charismatic salesperson? Often they take you completely unawares, striking up a regular conversation and sucking you in before you ever realize you might be pressed to purchase something a few minutes later.

The more engaged you became in the conversation, and the more likable they are, the more you feel almost obligated to at least hear them out. The next thing you know, you're trying out their food stand or buying a new TV.

So how does this happen? People are naturally drawn to charismatic members of society, even when they don't know them personally. So even if you're not on the ground selling to individuals, building your brand around a charismatic leader with great people skills can make a world of difference. Need an example? Consider Apple.

Marketing Tip 27: Offer Sponsorships

Many companies enjoy great promotional opportunities through sponsoring events, people, and teams. Associations with big events, popular charities, and local athletes can definitely bring in some great PR, and boost sales.

When sponsoring events, companies gain visibility by showcasing or selling their products at the event, or by adding their logos and big banners to the overall décor. When sponsoring people and teams, especially athletes, the company's logo is usually emblazoned on their equipment or the clothes they wear for the event.

By encouraging consumers to try the product at these events, the company reaches a new group of people who may love their product and become new and loyal customers. Even if people choose not to buy anything at these events, the company name and logo becomes more familiar. This may influence purchase decisions the next time they come across the product or service.

How to Sponsor an Event in Your Area

Organizing an event does not have to be difficult. Here's a simple guide to getting the ball rolling.

- Contact a charitable organization like the Red Cross and see about holding a blood drive or a related event.
- Contact a sporting charity and you can outsource organization for a marathon or field day that will bear your name and funding.
- Adopt an educational program like the ones offered by Kumon and Scholastic and open up your business to area families for an event day.
- Ask business associates to advertise your event.
- Use an email RSVP system to estimate the number of guests when you shop for amenities and snacks.

Marketing Tip 28: Build Relationships with Bulk Buyers

In the online marketing tips, I mentioned the importance of encouraging customers to buy more items using pricing. However, there are also some customers who buy in bulk because they have to, and it's time you found them. This takes a lot of searching and pitching, but if you can strike up a relationship and land a deal with such a buyer, then your sales will skyrocket.

Imagine that you own a company specializing in building custom-made PCs for individual customers who need computers for specific needs. This may include anything from gaming to use for school. A few blocks away, a financial consultancy firm is looking to upgrade all the equipment in the office. Imagine how landing that one deal can translate into maybe 25 orders, while continuing with individual customers brings in only one or two per person.

Marketing Tip 29: Set Up a Promotional Cartel

When most people think of cartels, they think of drugs and violence, but there are cartels that can promote a great deal of good for customers and everyone else involved. Have you ever followed a page on Twitter for humor or inspirational quotes, and then noticed that they spend a great deal of time promoting each other? This is a cartel built for promotional purposes.

Setting one up is easy. Simply contact other people in the industry and offer to promote their products and services for free, if they do the same for you. Local events and businesses often promote each other, even when they compete within the same industry. However, the best option is to promote a complementary service.

Marketing Tip 30: Pair Up and Form a Partnership

Building a partnership requires way more involvement than just cross-promoting. This calls for brands to work together on major projects, and may even lead to mergers or the formation of jointly owned subsidiaries. This happens all the time, but how does it work?

Say for instance you create a homemade spaghetti sauce that takes off in a local neighborhood and you have the chance to showcase how amazing it is at an event. There are other products you would need to make this happen, like kitchenware, pasta, garlic bread, and maybe even a dessert option, and wine.

Why not boost sales by partnering with manufacturers of these products, and even allowing them to set up booths nearby? Maybe you could partner with a local restaurant that makes a whole new item on the menu incorporating your sauce. Imagine how many jars you'll sell of that delicious homemade brew – far more than if you chose to promote your sauce alone.

Marketing Tip 31: Make It Easy to Chat

It takes a lot of time, effort, and sometimes money to build a strong brand reputation. But all it takes for that to come crashing down is a scandal that spreads like wildfire in a community, or in the media. Once this takes root, it is often difficult to dislodge. However, customers rarely just want to blindside companies with bad PR. Instead, it's bad customer service that usually sends them down this path.

To ensure great customer service, companies should start by making themselves easy to reach – whether by phone, email, social media, or online chat. This way, customers can ask pressing questions that may prevent them from making a bad purchase. If there is a problem post-sale then customers can also use this avenue to voice their discrepancies and have them privately resolved before it becomes a public issue.

Experts like Zopim can help by offering live chat options. How? It reduces the likelihood of potential customers abandoning items in their virtual shopping carts, and also increases the average value of each order. People tend to spend more money after a live chat, and may be more open to upgrade options.

Marketing Tip 32: Practice Social Media Listening and Community Management

Smart brands use social media listening to monitor and assess what people are saying about the company online, and in the public media. It may also be expanded to include what people are saying about that particular industry in general, or problems the brand and its products may be able to solve.

Through community management, you can harness what you learn from social media listening to form new connections with the right people. Community managers can then seek out and interact with these people, to boost awareness of the company, and to push the products and services as solutions to problems in the industry.

Marketing Tip 33: Collaborate with Industry Experts

Ever noticed how a lot of smaller artists get their moment in the spotlight through collaborations with more popular musicians? Well the same premise works just as well in business, especially when companies get the chance to work with iconic brands or charismatic leaders.

Working with industry experts helps to add credibility to the brand and its products and services. It also attracts the interest of consumers of other brands the industry expert may have worked on before, and this may lead to higher conversion rates. If the industry expert is well known in the media then this is also a great press opportunity to spread the word and boost visibility.

Marketing Tip 34: Attend Conferences, Seminars, and Exhibits

A great way to meet industry experts and to further boost the credibility of your products and services is to attend conferences, seminars, and exhibits in your field. This not only connects you with the right people, but also makes them aware of what you bring to the table. In addition to this, it provides a perfect opportunity to showcase what your product can do to an audience who has an interest in your line of expertise.

Even if there are no opportunities to directly sell your products and services, go for the experience and participate where possible. Give a speech, shake a few hands, get some contacts you can reach out to later, and share some business cards. You never know what connection can help you take things to the next level.

Marketing Tip 35: Accept Every Press Opportunity

Another great way to build good PR is to accept every press opportunity that comes your way, if possible. This means accepting even press opportunities from small blogs and YouTube channels. This helps to put more content out there about your products and services and allows you to reach the audience behind the interviewer, no matter how small.
It's hard to predict what may or may not go viral if there's no big marketing budget behind it. However, it's amazing how often a well-spoken (or even ill-spoken line) at just the right time can quickly become ingrained in pop culture when you least expect it.

Marketing Tip 36: Display Testimonials on the Website

A great way to build trust with new and potential customers is to prove how satisfied other customers have been with your work. To do this, you need only to display testimonials, preferably at the bottom of your home page. Testimonials work best when they include headshots, a name, title or company, and then the quote.

Some companies may also choose to post occasional testimonials on social media to showcase customer satisfaction. A great source for your first set of testimonials is from customers tweeting or commenting on Facebook posts to let you know how amazing your products and services have been. Share these posts, and secure their permission to include them on your website.

How to Display Testimonials

The best way to handle this is just like an FAQ page. Create a testimonial page and list the good things people say about your service and quality. It helps to put pictures beside the testimonials, as it humanizes the accounts of product use Also, place offer a contact form at the bottom of the page that will give the customer an opportunity to add to the testimonials.

Make sure you offer a checkable box asking for permission to post their testimonial on the page and to use it elsewhere for advertising purposes.

Marketing Tip 37: Focus on the Workforce

Most businesses focus so much on their external customers that there is little investment made in the internal customers. Keeping employees happy is just as important as pleasing buyers. This is especially true for employees who represent the face of the business. These may include front desk clerks, secretaries, customer service reps, cashiers, and sales reps. To keep employees happy, focus on the perks you can give that might not cost you a dime but make the world of difference. This may include flexible hours, greater autonomy over their work, personalized work spaces, and social events in the office or out as a team. Most importantly, however, focus on training the workforce.

A well trained force has all the skills and abilities needed to handle even the toughest tasks, and even in the face of pressure and scandal. Well trained employees also work better as a unit, since they learned the same procedures and value systems to tackle unique problems.

Marketing Tip 38: Turn Customers into Members

To strengthen relationships with customers, try turning customers into members. Many companies try to do this by forcing customers to create accounts to do simple things like read important information or make a purchase. This is not a good idea.

Rather than provide restrictions compelling customers to become members, provide incentives. Incentives might include members-only discounts; special coupons; first preference for limited inventory; even beta testing of new products, services, and features. These incentives help to boost recurring sales and product loyalty.

Setting up a membership site is a lot more complicated than regular website building and may require closer monitoring and administrative work. To make the process easier, WordPress users should consider using membership plugins. Companies can also consider enabling settings on the site that allow people to sign in with other social media credentials like Google or Facebook.

Marketing Tip 39: Take a Monetary Loss over the Loss of a Customer

Some companies like to play hardball when it comes to refunds and returns. This saves them money in the short term, but in the long run, it costs them. That customer is unlikely to try any other product from the company again, and will likely discourage family and friends from doing so.

The ideal response is to allow the customer to keep the product and to issue a full refund. If you genuinely cannot afford this, then accept the returned product and issue a full or partial refund. The customer will remember your willingness to accept the loss, and if allowed to keep the product, may actually grow fond of it over time and return to purchase other goods.

Marketing Tip 40: Issue Surveys

The best way to boost sales is to give your customers exactly what they want, and the best way to find out what they want is to ask. But how do you get this information from a large number of customers in order to use that information to improve marketing and sales? Easy! Set up a short survey with no more than ten questions.

To encourage customers to take these surveys, provide incentives. Incentives might include a certain dollar value off their next purchase, a 10% discount, or even the opportunity to have their 'testimonials' featured on the website, should they provide one.

How Do You Make a Survey?

Sites like Free Online Survey provide an easy way to create and host surveys, and the surveys can be embedded in your own website just by copy-and-pasting them from the "embed" function on the survey host site. It's simple to use these survey sites to record customer experiences and even to harvest more testimonials.

This free video (click on the link below) from Typeform will explain in more depth how easy it is to make a survey online.

http://referral.typeform.com/mzbLei8

5 AUDIO-VISUAL TIPS TO BOOST SALES

Twitter is reminiscent of a time when words were king in the world of content creation. However, the popularity of memes, and social media platforms like Pinterest and Instagram, swiftly changed that.

Now more and more companies look to pictures, videos, and GIFS to brand their products and services, and more importantly, improve sales.

So what can you do to help your audio-visual promotions stand out from the rest? And how can you use videos to improve sales? By making them popular and ensuring your brand gets a moment in the spotlight. Here's how.

Marketing Tip 41: Take Advantage of Pop Culture References

When making and marketing videos, capitalizing on pop culture references and trending topics can help boost its popularity. When something big is happening in the media, people want to consume more and more material on that specific topic, and this makes them more likely to view the video.

Try to include these references in a seamless way that does not take away from the point, and ensure the references are relevant. Unless you feel strongly about a particular issue, at whatever cost stay away from controversial topics that may alienate some of your customers like religion, race, sexuality, and politics.

Marketing Tip 42: Use a Professional Script for Ads

Some artists can improvise on a creative project and create a masterpiece. There have been entire movies filmed without a script, where the director called on the actors to get into character and improvise. Sometimes this works, but often it does not. Don't take the risk. Get a professional to work on a script that reads well, and translates well on screen.

The script should include not just the lines of the actors involved, but also information on the setting, and how the characters should look and dress. This helps to ensure diversity in the ads to appeal to a larger demographic.

Marketing Tip 43: Pull a Publicity Stunt

Even when a professional script is involved, not every ad needs to be an obvious one, and not every ad needs to be high quality. Think of all the low quality videos looking like shots made by passersby that turned out to be nothing but publicity stunts. Making a video that's funny, shocking, or inspiring can attract a large audience and encourage people to share the content.

Publicity stunts don't always include videos though. It could include public appearances, big art installments appearing in the middle of the night, or making a difficult personal pledge and sticking to it. Get thinking, get creative, and put it out there. If it's good enough, other people will record it and spread it for you!

Marketing Tip 44: Hire a Celebrity to Be Your Spokesperson

This may sound out of your budget, but a celebrity doesn't always mean a Taylor Swift or Justin Bieber. There are many familiar faces in local neighborhoods, niche markets, and online communities that would love the opportunity to become brand ambassadors for the right company. All you need to do is find one.

Great candidates include local athletes or entire teams, politicians, popular faces, well-established families, or the owner of a popular business. For instance, if you're pushing a new brand of athletic wear, who better to endorse it in a video than the local football team?

How Do You Find and Hire a Celebrity?

Contacting a celebrity directly is next to impossible. You're going to want to start with publicists and talent agents. Call up an agency, ask who's available, or for a specific represented celebrity you've already got in mind, and then figure out price and schedule. The real limiting factors here are money and celebrity schedules.

Marketing Tip 45: Make Product Reviews

A great way to boost sales with audio-visual content is to make product reviews. The company can review the product on their own and include information on the specs, as well as answers to frequently asked questions. Even more impactful, however, is sending out free samples to key influencers who can then post videos on YouTube and link to them in sections where your product is for sale.

3 PRINT MEDIA TIPS FOR BOOSTING SALES

Print media is quickly going out of style, but it isn't gone just yet. In fact, there are still many great ways to use print media to boost sales and help with branding. Here are a few.

Marketing Tip 46: Get it Made by a Professional

Whether it's a business card, a magazine, or a flier, get it made by a professional. This increases the likelihood of a great, coherent design that will catch the eye of customers. The quality of the print media also reflects on the quality of the brand and its products and services.

There are plenty of places on the internet where you can get things made for you. Banners, Book Covers and so much money. Upwork and Fiverr are just two of the many websites that you can use.

Click below to see what you can get made on Fiverr.

http://tracking.fiverr.com/SH2YF

Marketing Tip 47: Include Coupons

Once you've made it attractive enough to get their attention, the next step is to make the print media valuable enough, and worth keeping. The easiest way to make it valuable is to add coupons either at the end, or the back. These coupons encourage purchases from customers who might not have otherwise thought to buy your products and services.

Marketing Tip 48: Include Business Information

Even with coupons, some people might still be reluctant to make a purchase because they have outstanding questions. Provide an avenue for communication by including business information like customer service and your website information. If you don't have a website, then include the company's Facebook page, and other social media pages.

Throughout this book, we've showed how to use online marketing, videos, print media, and networking to boost sales. However, whether a product or service sells or not often depends on the product itself. Sometimes no amount of marketing can account for defects in the product. So along with ensuring your product or service meets the best possible standards, here are two more ways to help you boost sales.

2 PRODUCT TIPS TO BOOST SALES

Marketing Tip 49: Make it Hands-Free and Easy to Use

Making sales is one thing, but being able to charge a premium price is even better! The more hands free you make a product or service, then the more you can charge. This doesn't always involve a lot of extra work on your part. It might mean extra features for a premium account on an app that automatically becomes unlocked when the package is bought. It could also mean doing some SEO optimization for an article that may take ten minutes and cost an extra $20.

Marketing Tip 50: Make it Exclusive

Every business wants to improve sales, but improving sales is relative to how many items there are for sale. By making an item exclusive, you limit how much of a particular item is sold. This seems contradictory to making a profit, until you consider Rolex's business model, and that of so many other luxury brands.

Rolex is known for making high-end watches with a price to match. And rather than depreciating in value over time, these watches actually become more and more valuable and expensive. But how? Rolex makes only a certain number of watches per model, making them exclusive and allowing them to keep the price high.

There are several ways to mirror this. You can make your entire roster of offerings exclusive and therefore high priced. Or you can make just select items limited edition or seasonal. Another option is to create a subsidiary of more high-end products. Whatever option you choose, remember exclusivity also requires great quality to justify high prices.

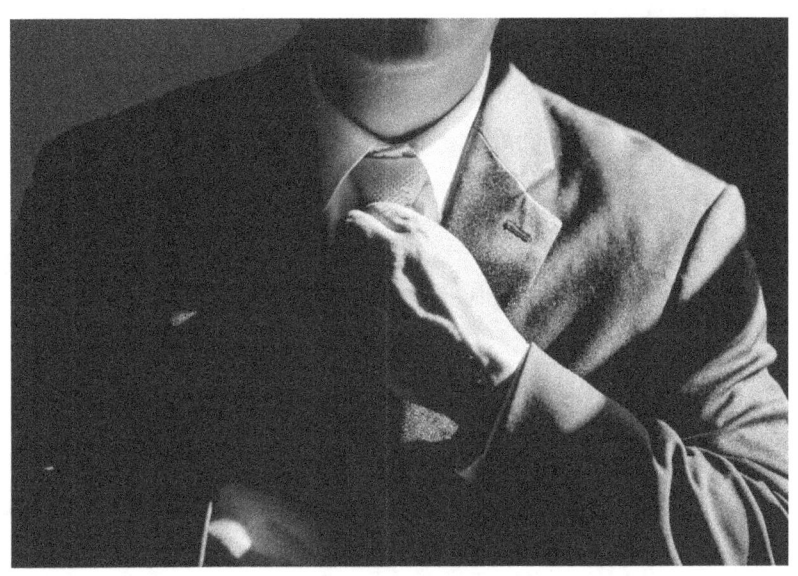

CONCLUSION

Marketing and public relations work hand-in-hand to boost sales through a number of avenues in areas of online marketing, video productions, networking, print media, and product innovations. Some of these tips lead to immediate results in boosted sales, while others take a longer time to manifest. Patience and consistency are key.

In today's digital age, online marketing shows the greatest promise of boosting sales through marketing and PR. The online community is vast and allows brands to reach customers all around the world with the click of a button. Through great SEO practices, it also allows customers to find companies that meet their needs, and solves their problems.

Networking and building relationships perhaps requires the greatest time investment of all the different mediums to boost sales. However, who you know and who knows you is also one of the greatest keys to success in the business world, and therefore worth the effort and worth the wait.

In spite of the popularity of online marketing, and the impact of networking, video production has steadily become a force to be reckoned with. This is true whether the videos make it onto billboard's, get stuffed in-between your favorite TV shows, get shared on iChat, or spread virally online. Videos are often more appealing to viewers than text as it stimulates more of their senses, and leaves very little to the imagination.

Almost obsolete, print media nonetheless continues to hold significance to promote products and services and boost sales. Web pages often get closed and forgotten, and social media posts often get shuffled down the timeline. But tangible media endures.

Finally, the actual product and service can often provide the key to boosting sales through providing value, ease of use, and a sense of exclusivity.

www.ingramcontent.com/pod-product-compliance
Lightning Source LLC
Chambersburg PA
CBHW072228170526
45158CB00002BA/806